SUPERSTITION AND FOLKLORE
OF THE
WEST COUNTRY

DORSET, DEVON & SOMERSET

Written by M. Dudridge

Drawings by:
Kate Mayely and Lindsey Greenhill

ISBN No: 0 907683 13 4

Published: Nigel J. Clarke Publications
Tappers Knapp,
Lyme Regis,
Dorset.

GW00673588

INDEX

2

SUPERSTITION AND FOLKLORE OF THE WEST COUNTRY

A brief account of some of the legends and beliefs to be found in Devon, Dorset and Somerset.

FOLKLORE AND SUPERSTITION IN THE WEST COUNTRY

'Folklore and Superstition in Old Wessex' is a very brief account of some of the ancient stories, customs and beliefs that can be found in the villages and towns between Poole, Exeter and Honiton, and over the border into Somerset as far as Haselbury Plucknett and Hinton St. George. There are many curious traditions and festivals faithfully enjoyed to the present day in areas where the participants have long forgotten the meanings of the rituals they still treasure, and many mysterious tales still recounted with relish when the curtains are closed and chairs drawn up to the fire.

4

WHAT IS FOLKLORE?

Old habits and customs are disappearing rapidly in our modern world of science and the computer, yet they die hard. Beneath our new sophistication still lurk the echoes of older beliefs. Ancient remedies for sickness, strange traditions whose origins are lost in the mists of time, can still be found in the quiet villages of Dorset, Devon and Somerset, some of them indeed traceable right back to our Celtic ancestors of more than two thousand years ago and the old gods they worshipped then. The arrival of Christianity to our shores brought changes of course, and new ways that have themselves now become part of our rich heritage of folklore. Strange customs still abound at the great Christian festivals of Christmas and Easter. Special foods are eaten, such as pancakes on Shrove Tuesday, which owe their origins directly to the laws and prohibitions of the newly arrived faith. It was the need for the housewife to clear the larder of luxury foods like eggs before the penitential season of Lent that made some inventive cook whip up the first pancake, so that shriven of sin and with a cupboard bare of temptation, the Christian could approach Easter in a true spirit .... "A sad tale's best for winter. I have one of sprites and goblins...." so said the little little prince in Shakespeare's 'A Winter's Tale', but sad or happy, there are many tales in the West Country of supernatural happenings that spring from the history of the place and the people who have lived here through the centuries. Heroes and villains of long ago have all left their mark on the folklore of Old Wessex. But still, it was Christianity that was the single greatest catalyst in the history of our land. This new faith was to alter completely the world of the ancient Celtic tries, and turn their old gods of yesterday into the devils of today.

WESSEX AND THE DEVIL

In Old Wessex there are a great many stories about the Devil and his works. Huge piles of ancient rocks testify to contests he had with local holy men and saints, and his eventual, inevitable defeat at their hands. Standing stones still bear his name, and many a West Country church has been erected by gallant Christian villagers in the very teeth of his infernal opposition.

At Honiton the contest with the Devil led to stones being thrown, but he failed to prevent the church being built, and the Devil's Stone on Church Hill remains to bear witness to the fight. Portesham, a small village between Abbotsbury and Weymouth, has a chamber tomb which has been given rise to a devil legend. The stones of the tomb were thought to have been thrown by Satan when he was indulging in one of his favourite sports, playing quoits. In this case, he threw the stones from Portland, approximately ten miles off.

The Devil and the 9 Stones

Nine Stones at Winterbourne Abbas

Further north at Winterborne Abbas, a neat little circle of stones lies right beside the A35. This circle has several names, including The Devil's Nine Stones and The Devil, His Wife and Children. Legend has it that they were children turned into stone for playing fivestones on the Sabbath.

7

Simon's Barrow

Away across the county border, in the Blackdown Hills of Somerset, lies The Devil's Lapful. This is a pile of stones that the Devil collected in order to prevent the building of Wellington Church. He put them in his leather apron to carry, but the straps broke and the stones were scattered. A few that he held in his glove lay separately and became known as The Devil's Glove. The large group, Simon's Barrow, and the smaller group, were always safe, for whoever tried to steal the stones for building purposes found that the Devil returned them promptly to their proper resting place.

STONES OF MYSTERY AND LEGEND

Before the skills of modern archaeology enabled us to learn more about the stone circles and burial mounds scattered around the countryside, it was natural for our forebears to weave stories around them in an attempt to explain their presence. The Devil legends are some of these, but other tales grew up around the old stones, telling of magical happenings and crocks of gold, that served to increase their mystery in the eyes of country folk.

A Ghostly Army

Flowers barrow at East Lulworth is an ancient hill fort. In December 1678 a 'great noise and clashing of arms' was heard coming from the area, and a spectral army was seen. As a result of this vision, the locals made some preparations for their own defence, but it was subsequently decided that the whole thing had been a mirage. Later on a gigantic skeleton was found in the vicinity.

Fairy Music

There are a number of barrows in Dorset where fairy music can be heard by listeners sitting at the top at midday. Bincombe and Whitcombe both have these Music Barrows, the melodies supposed to be from the fairies who live underneath them.

Ninebarrow Down and Slaughter Barrow

Ninebarrow Down at Corfe Castle and Slaughter Barrow at Gillingham both have links with the days of battle before the Norman Conquest. Ninebarrow is thought by local people to hold the burial places of nine kings killed in battle, and Slaughter Barrow contains the bodies of men also killed in a battle, but here it is dated more precisely as a battle between Saxons and Danes. So many died in that battle that blood flowed for a quarter of a mile.

Near to Bere Regis is a hill fort known as Woodbury Hill. It is the 'Green Hill' of Thomas Hardy's famous novel 'Far from the Madding Crowd' and contains the Anchoret's Well, in which legend has it there is a golden table or tablet. A famous fair was held here for centuries, and on September 21st each year folk would come to the Anchoret's Well to drink the waters which were thought to have healing properties.

HOLY WELLS

Apart from the Anchoret's Well, there are several other springs that are reputed to have healing properties in the western part of Dorset. Near to Bridport are two villages that have wells whose waters are supposed to heal sore eyes. Symondsbury water must be taken at the exact moment it is touched by the rays of the rising sun, although at Walditch there are no such requirements. Morecombelake, just off the

A35 road opposite the Ship Inn has an ancient spring associated with St. Wite. Some say that the mysterious saint who is the patron of the lovely old church at Whitchurch Canonicorum used the water from this spring for her healing. True or no, it is certain that the periwinkles on Stonebarrow Hill are linked with the Latin version of St. Wite's name. They are called St. Candida's Eyes.

St. Austin's Well

Near to Cerne Abbas is a well connected with the great St. Augustine. It reputedly sprang from the ground when the saint and his followers were being chased from the town after they had defeated the pagan god Heil. The wicked townsfolk pinned tails to the holy men and as a punishment for their behaviour, it was thought for generations after that Cerne folk were born with tails. The well was always thought to have healing properties.

LONG LEGGITY BEASTIES

Animals abound in folklore, and Old Wessex has its share. Cats, dogs and even rabbits have their tales. The dog is arguably the most common and there are many stories about them, particularly black dogs. Canon Doyle wrote about one in his famous 'Hound of the Baskervilles' and there are many local legends of fierce ghostly creatures that appear to the unwary in quiet lanes and deserted churchyards.

It is possible that there could be a link between some of these tales and the traditional 'Churchyard Grim'. In past years it was quite a common occurrence for a dog, preferably black, to be killed and buried on the north side of a churchyard so that its ghost could protect the inmates from the Devil. This belief was so widespread that there are a number of tales about ghostly black dogs, and several pubs are named after them.

The Black Dog at Uplyme, Devon

The current legends about this particular apparition seem to fall naturally into two parts, the inside dog and the outside one.

Although the present hotel is a comparatively recent building, the old Black Dog Inn was an old coaching inn of cob and thatch which fell into dilapidation some time before the First World War. The story goes that one of the upper rooms of the inn was occupied by an old man, possibly a miser, for he kept his money with him in a pot. His only companion was a dog. Thieves broke into his room one day, but the old man did not divulge the whereabouts of his money. The robbers killed him but went away empty-handed, leaving the black dog to mourn for his master, pining away at the foot of the stairs. For many years, the owner took no notice of the ghostly animal that sat by his fireside until one day he decided on impulse to chase it away with a poker. The apparition leapt out of range and made a bound for the ceiling, doing a considerable amount of damage. It was during repairs that a pot of coins was discovered dating from the time of Charles I. After this the dog disappeared from the inn and was thought to confine its activities to the lane behind. The present landlady assures me that neither she nor her family have ever sensed anything supernatural in the present building.

The outdoor dog is a monstrous black creature that appears in Black Dog Lane behind the hotel. It gets larger and larger, and seeing it is supposed to foretell the death of the unfortunate beholder. One version claims that if the victim of this unpleasant apparition can retain enough presence of mind to toss a coin to the dog it will disappear, but as it has not been seen within living memory, there is no way of knowing whether the notion works!

A jumping black dog haunts the Swyre-Puncknowle road, and an old lady in Bridport in 1915 told of a 'girt black dog so big as a donkey'. The apparition disappeared, and when the lady returned to her home she found that her child had died in her absence. She said then that she knew the dog had been a portent, but not that it was to do with her own daughter.

Black dogs have also been seen at Chideock, Beaminster and Charmouth. Portland has its Roy Dog, or as it is sometimes known, the Row (to rhyme with cow) Dog. This too was a shaggy creature, as tall as a man, with eyes as big as plates. Whilst it did not actually attack its victim, it proved an unpleasant barrier, and has been seen in many different parts of the island. It is traditionally thought to have its home in Cave Hole, a pothole in the rocks not far from Portland Bill which opens into a large cavern.

Portland has an interesting taboo about rabbits. It is thought amongst islanders that rabbits caused a great deal of damage to the quarries with their constant burrowing, and indeed, the little creatures have been blamed for more than one fatal accident. As a result it is just not done to mention the word 'rabbit'. There may be some truth in the idea that the rabbits do damage the workings, but it could also be a partial remembrance of some pagan connection that has been passed down through the island folk memory.

The monster cat of Sturminster Newton

Near the castle ruins at the top of Newton Hill there is a place called The Hollow, and it is here that legend has it a monster cat has been seen. A great black creature with huge eyes, it is supposed to run on a track parallel to the main road, but this is a very old story and nobody in the vicinity now knows anything about it. There are also vague stories of a cat in the Shillingstone area but nothing at all is known about it now.

TRADITIONS AND CUSTOMS

Many old customs still linger, and traditions that have their roots firmly in the past are still carried out in the quiet farms and villages of Old Wessex. Ceremonies to ensure a good harvest, or to obtain a good husband for an unmarried girl still abound, as well as others like maypole dancing and tar barrel rolling that are just good fun.

St. Katharine's Chapel at Abbotsbury

St. Katharine's Chapel at Abbotsbury and St. Katharine's Chapel near Cerne Abbas are both dedicated to the kindly saint who tries to find husbands for local unmarried girls. They go to her and pray for a husband with the following rhyme:

Sweet St. Katharine send me a husband,

A good one I pray:

But better arn a one than narn a one.

Oh, St. Katharine
Lend me thine aid
And grant that I never may
Die an old maid.

"Here we come a-wassailing ...."

For centuries, cider has been an important part of the Wessex economy, and there are a number of ceremonies attached to the making of the brew and the growing of the apples. In Devon and Somerset the orchards are 'wassailed' in order to ensure a good crop of fruit in the coming season. On Twelfth Night, or perhaps more usually Old Twelfth Night (17th January) the farmer and his family and friends regale themselves on hot cakes and cider, and then make their way down to the orchards after dark for the ceremony. They choose a tree, generally the oldest one, and greet the good spirits by putting a piece of toast or a cake soaked in cider among the branches, then tossing more cider on the ground as a libation. In order to scare off the evil spirits, the men fire guns into the boughs and bang on kettles and pots, and the others in the party bow and sing the Wassail Song.

Here's to thee, old apple tree,
Whence thou may'st bud and whence thou may'st blow!
And whence thou may'st bear apples enow.
Hatsfull! Capsfull!
Bushell-bushell-sacksfull!
And my pockets full too! Huzza!

Football in Purbeck

On Shrove Tuesday each year, quarrymen from the area of Corfe Castle keep open their old right of way to Swanage Harbour by kicking a ball in the direction of Swanage. The last to have been married during the past year has to provide the football.

Lent Crocking

This custom has come into disrepute because there is generally some damage, but in past years on Shrove Tuesday, or Pansharding Day, small boys would go in groups from door to door of their village, carrying with them a stock of brocken pottery. The leader would knock at the doors and chant the following rhyme:

I be come a-shrovin'
For a little pancake
A bit o' bread o' your bakin'
Or a little truckle cheese o' your own makin'
If you'll give me a little I'll ax no more,
If you don't give me nothin' I'll rottle your door!

This seems to have something in common with the American custom of 'Trick or Treat', with its threat of reprisal if the unfortunate houseowner doesn't provide the goodies asked for!

Abbotsbury Garland Day

May 1st, of course, was a holiday long before Labour Day was even heard of, and maypoles have for centuries been a feature of English village greens. In Kingsteignton, Devon, maypole dancing is still performed on this day, and twelve days later, on 'Old May Day' in Abbotsbury, the villagers celebrate the start of summer with their Garland Day. On May 13th, the children of the village make garlands of flowers and go from house to house collecting money. The whole village takes part in the festivities, and years ago, the childrens' wreaths were placed in local fishing boats and taken out to sea to be tossed into the water to ensure a good harvest of fish. There are few boats left now, so the garlands go round the War Memorial and the money collected is shared amongst the children.

Bonfire Night

Bonfire Night on November 5th is as well-known to children today as it has been to those of the past three hundred and eighty years. There can be very few who are unable to chant the old rhyme which tells the story of the ill-fated Guy Fawkes and his Gunpowder Plot.

> Please to remember the fifth of November,
> Gunpowder treason and plot.
> I see no reason why gunpowder treason should ever be forgot.

Guy and his fellow conspirators did not succeed in blowing up the Houses of Parliament, but their attempt, and their terrible fate, have been remembered ever since with bonfires, stuffed 'guys' to burn on the top, and fireworks.

Barrels and Boulders

In Ottery St. Mary, Devon, they have given the old customs a different twist. Fiery barrels, each one sponsored by a local pub, are carried on the shoulders of men who run in groups through the crowds. This was also done in Bridgwater until it was considered too dangerous, so now the barrels are either rolled or pushed on sledges.

In Shebbear, North Devon, the prosperity of the village is ensured for the coming year with the old custom of 'turning the boulder.' The Devil's Boulder lies under an oak tree in the square, and each November 5th the villagers give it a heave, and the church bell is rung, to make sure that the next year will be a good one.

Skimmington Riding

Skimmington riding, or 'rough music' as is was sometimes called, was designed to express the disapproval of a community against any of their number who offended against the local code of morals. It was known in the eighteenth century and Thomas Hardy describes it in 'The Mayor of Casterbridge'. A lifelike dummy of the victim, be it henpecked husband or a couple known to be behaving improperly, would

16

be paraded through the village accompanied by villagers banging on pots and pans. A skimmer was a likely drumstick, so giving the event its name. This might be done two or three nights in succession, and possibly on the last night the figures would be burned in front of the house of the victims. Such public condemnation would have been designed to shame the unfortunate person who had transgressed, but even in the days of Hardy this cruel custom was falling into disuse.

LEGENDS OF CHRISTMAS

Countless legends and stories have accrued throughout the past two thousand years around the birth of Jesus. But there are many traditions, too, that were from the even earlier Celtic and Nordic feasts of winter. To our pagan ancestors, the sun meant life, and in the dark of the year it was necessary

17

to remind themselves that the days were once more going to lengthen and that spring would return to the earth. Yule was the old Nordic term for the winter solstice, and this became incorporated by incoming Christians into their celebrations of the birth of Christ.

The Ashen Faggot

In Devon and Somerset the traditional Yule Log is replaced by the 'Ashen Faggot', a mass of twigs and small branches picked green from the tree and bound with reeds or withies. This was pulled into the hearth and lit. Some traditions have it that unmarried girls each chose a withy to watch. The first one to burn through meant that the girl who had chosen it would be the first to marry. Certainly a fresh round of cider is consumed as each bond snaps.

The old reason for choosing ash for the faggot is that legend has it that Mary and Joseph used that wood for their fire on the very first Christmas, but the ash does have a history of being a tree with special properties. It was used in the curing of warts and for children with hernias or rickets. The 'Ashen Faggot' is to be found in many parts of Old Wessex, and its burning is accompanied by a great deal of cider drinking and conviviality.

The Kissing Bush

As the 'Ashen Faggot' was a substitute for the Yule Log, so the 'Kissing Bush' was a substitute for mistletoe. It was a small branch or bush of holly or yew dipped in water and dusted with flour to resemble snow. This was hung from the ceiling with decorations of apples, berries and gaily wrapped sweetmeats.

On the borders of Somerset and Dorset girls pull the berries off sprays of mistletoe, but have to try not to let anyone see them do it. If they are spotted, they are in danger of being chased and kissed — as many times as there were berries!

Symondsbury Mummers

Mummers have been popular for more than a thousand years, and although there are not many groups left, the tradition is still strong in the little village of Symondsbury, West Dorset. The time-honoured theme of the fight between St. George and his foreign adversary, in this case the King of Egypt, is followed by the Doctor bringing all the saintly characters, including St. Patrick and Valentine, back to life. A Dame, a Horse, Captain Bluster and Colonel Spring all take part, the saints and warriors carrying swords and all wearing tall headdresses with coloured paper streamers that cover their faces. Performances are often in the grounds of pubs during the Christmas holiday period — a splendid traditional custom that is still being enjoyed.

Holly Riders

In the remoter districts of Somerset, Holly Riders were a feature of the Christmas celebrations. Wearing holly in their buttonholes and around their hats, they would ride from house to house singing carols in return for cakes and cider. In the early years of the nineteenth century in Exeter, church choirs would spend most of Christmas Eve night carol singing, only returning to the Cathedral at about six o'clock Christmas morning in time for morning service at seven.

Ilminster's Holy Thorn

There is a tale of an Ilminster pilgrim and how he brought back to his home a slip of the famous Holy Thorn from the Abbey of Glastonbury. None of his friends believed it could really be a Holy Thorn, but the pilgrim planted it and prayed that it would flower at Christmas. December 25th passed and it seemed as though he had been wrong, but then, on the evening of January 5th, Old Christmas Eve, villagers were awakened by the sound of hooves in the street.

Looking from their windows they were amazed to see all the local animals clattering down the road to where the little thorn tree grew. Quickly they dressed and followed. The pilgrim was already kneeling in prayer, and as the church bell struck midnight the animals did the same, bending before the tiny tree now white with blossom.

'Eating a Christmas Pie ....'

There are so many traditions and tales about Christmas food it is a wonder we have appetites for the remaining eleven months of the year! Mincemeat, which used to contain meat but now is a mixture of dried fruits, suet and apples, is a perennial favourite, and it is considered unlucky to refuse a mince pie, even if you are already full! To eat one for every month of the year is to ensure good luck, and to reject one is to invite ill fortune.

Frumenty (pronounced frummity) used to be eaten in many places as a traditional part of the Christmas celebrations, and it is particularly associated with Wessex. It was this mixture of boiled wheat well-laced with rum that left Michael Henchard so intoxicated that he took advantage of another ancient Dorset custom and sold his wife, Susan! With the money he set himself up in business in Casterbridge and ended up as Mayor. Thomas Hardy was clearly familiar with this ancient dish. In Devon there is a drink that was very popular known as egg-hot. It consisted of cider warmed with eggs and spices. A strongly spiced kind of punch was drunk from the wassail bowl — or perhaps 'lambswool' a mixture of ale and spices and roasted apples, preferably crabapples. Shakespeare refers to this when Puck says in "A Midsummer Night's Dream",

"And sometime lurk I in a gossip's bowl,
In very likeness of a roasted crab — "

FESTIVALS OF THE CELTIC YEAR

Our Celtic ancestors had four great festivals, Beltane in May, Lugnasadh in August, Samhain in November and Imbolc in February. These were taken over at the coming on Christianity, so that now Lugnasadh is more familiar as Lammas or 'Loaf Mass', when the harvesting of the first fruits is honoured, and Samhain, the ancient Festival of the Dead, has become known as All Souls' Night or Hallowe'en.

Exeter's Lammas Fair

For more than a thousand years, Exeter held a great fair in late July. Called *hlafmesse* by the Saxons, the Lammas Fair was only one of several great fairs held in the city, but sadly, it has now been discontinued. It was proclaimed by the Mayor at the Guildhall, and he and other City dignitories walked in procession behind a large white glove that topped a pole decorated with ribbons and flowers. After the proclamation, this was hoisted to the roof of the Guildhall for the duration of the fair. The glove was important, as it was a symbol of the royal protection of the peace and a sign that throughout the period it was displayed, outsiders could enter the city and trade at the fair. No man could be arrested whilst the fair was on, although the immunity was only for debt and not for more serious offences.

In 1964 it was decided that the procession caused too much traffic disruption, but in order to maintain an ancient tradition, the proclamation is still made from the Guildhall on the Tuesday before the third Wednesday in July. Indeed, in 1983, the Mayor went in the former Sheriff's coach from the Civic Centre to the Guildhall where he read the Proclamation and the glove was hoisted at noon. Then he returned to Dix's Field by the Civic Centre and was entertained by costumed children dancing around a maypole.

Hot Penny Ceremony at Honiton

This ceremony has no known connection with Lammas, but it does have striking similarities with Exeter's tradition. On the Tuesday after July 19th, the Town Crier in full regalia carries a gilded glove on high as a symbol that a market is about to begin. The procession goes from the White Lion at one end of the town to The Angel at the other, and the glove is hoisted on each inn in alternate years, with the following cry:

Oyez! Oyez! Oyez!

The Glove is up and the Fair is open

No man shall be arrested until the Glove is taken down.

God Save the Queen!

The glove is then placed over the inn porch and hot pennies are thrown for children to scramble for.

Still, in some parts of Devonshire, loaves known as 'Lammas Bread' are made from the first threshings of corn, and farmers break them up and scatter the pieces in the corners of their barn.

Punkie Night at Hinton St. George

Hinton St. George, a village near Crewkerne, celebrates All Souls' Night or Hallowe'en with Punkie Night. This is the evening when the local children parade with lanterns or punkies made out of hollowed turnips or mangel-worzels which they have designed themselves. The procession is headed by the Punkie King and Queen, and they walk through the village singing:

It's Punkie Night, it's Punkie Night,

Give us a candle, give us a light.

If you don't, you'll get a fright.

Another song is also heard on Hallowe'en. Older villagers still call it 'soul singing' for dead friends and relatives.

A soul, a soul for a soul cake,
One for Jack Smith
And one for Tom White
And one for myself and I'll bid you goodnight.
My clothes are very ragged
My shoes are very thin
I've got a little pocket to put three halfpence in
And I'll never come a-souling until another year.

To the Celts, the last night in October symbolised the Festival of the Dead, and their feast of Samhain was associated with the dying of the year.

Before the gods that made the gods
Had seen their sunrise pass,
The White Horse of the White Horse Vale
Was cut out of the grass

G. K. Chesterton

MISCELLANY

The Bridport Dagger

For centuries now, as far back as the days of King John of Magna Carta fame, Bridport has been a major centre of the rope-making trade. The town has provided ropes and nets for fishing and trapping, for lashing King Henry VIII's massive guns to the decks of his warships, and for sports such as tennis and cricket. Bridport ropes were also used at public executions. Their grimly humorous nickname was 'The Bridport Dagger' and it is interesting that John Leland, who travelled England between the years 1534 and 1543 remarked in his papers, 'At Bridport be made good daggers.' The wry wit of a local perhaps, unable to resist the opportunity of taking the rise out of the traveller!

The Duel of Charmouth

In 1792 the old house of Langmoor was occupied by an irascible veteran of a number of naval engagements with the French, a Lieutenant James Warden of His Majesty's Navy. Warden had various disagreements with neighbours about different matters, finally having a violent argument with a Charmouth resident called Norman Bond in Charmouth Street. Warden threatened to shoot Bond's dogs, and Bond retorted that he would not argue in the street. Warden responded by saying he would meet him in any way he chose, and the result was a challenge to a duel. It took place on the 28th April, 1792 between Charmouth and Axminster at Hunter's Lodge. Warden shot first but the ball went through Bond's hat harmlessly. Bond's shot came next and he killed his man. There was an inquest at Axminster and Bond was forced to seek refuge in Barbados for a while as duelling was frowned upon by the authorities.

The Hermit of Haselbury Plucknett

There were many occasions when the Devil had a pretty rough ride in Wessex. Certainly things did not go his way when he encountered the holy Saint Wulfric. It seems that Satan bought the soul of a poor man in the vicinity of Haselbury Plucknett, but his victim had second thoughts later about the bargain and ran away, hotly pursued by the aggrieved Devil. They reached the ford, where the man hoped to lose his pursuer as the Devil cannot cross water. However, Satan managed to grasp at his heel, and there they stayed. Now Haselbury Plucknett was the village where Saint Wulfric had a cell, and he was shown in a vision the poor man held at the ford. Armed with a Cross, the saint hastened to the rescue and sprinkled holy water over the Devil, who let out a terrible cry and made off.

Conjuring Minterne of Batcombe

Less saintly perhaps than Wulfric was the man known as Conjuring Minterne. John Minterne was squire of Batcombe, and local opinion held that he trafficked with the Devil. Now the church at Batcombe had four small pinnacles, but only three of them were properly in place, and the story goes that Conjuring Minterne jumped his horse from the nearby hill right over the tower and down into the village, knocking off that fourth pinnacle with his horse's hoof. It is not altogether surprising that the astounded villagers attributed his prowess to the Devil!

But of course, it is quite easy to get rid of the Devil, as any good Somerset dweller will tell you. Just throw a pinch of salt over your left shoulder and hit him in the eye!

The Rebel of Marlpits Hill, Honiton.

This legend dates from 1904, when a group of children accompanied by their schoolteacher were walking up the hill. The children all claimed to see a man coming towards them dressed in funny old-fashioned clothes and a wide-brimmed black hat. The children were frightened at the man's dishevelled appearance and the odd dazed stare on his face but the teacher could see nothing. Curious that they all seemed so convinced, she set enquiries in motion and discovered that after the Monmouth Rebellion in 1685 one of the rebels returned to his cottage at the top of Marlpits Hill. Just as his wife and children came out thankfully to greet him, a troop of the Royalist cavalry rode up and cut the rebel down with their swords before his family's eyes. At least one other sighting has been made of this man.

The Screaming Smuggler of Worbarrow Bay

When smuggling was at its height along the coast of Dorset there were many clashes between the smugglers and the Revenue Men. One evening near

Worbarrow Bay, a long smuggler was spotted and chased. He did not know the area and soon found his way blocked by an unscaleable cliff. Desperate, he fled into the sea. From the shore the Revenue men threw stones at him until he eventually died. Legend has it that when the moon is on the wane the sound os ghostly screams and splashes as the smuggler thrashes about in the water is heard by passers-by.

The Dragon of Kilve, Somerset.

Many legends surround the mystery of the formation of fossils, many have been tainted with quasi religious explanations. Kilve in Somerset is an area where a large number of fossils have been found, among which was the fossil of an Ichthyosaur (which from the latin translates as 'fish lizard'). At Kilve they tell the story of Blue Ben, who lived in a cave on nearby Potsham Hill, and would cool himself off in the waters of the Seven. The Devil found where Blue lived and would catch and harness the dragon to ride round hell. After one such excursion, Blue, hot and weary decided to bath in the waters of the Seven. While walking out into the sea, on the rocky outcrop of ledges the tired dragon slipt and fell into the mud, his remains fossilised in the rock.

The Trumpet Major's Hand

There are two stories to account for the haunting of Pimperne churchyard by the severed hand of a trumpet-major of dragoons. One dates back to the time of the Civil War, to a skirmish between some Roundheads and Cavaliers. The trumpet-major was captured by the villagers who supported the other side and as punishment they cut off his hand. When his comrades took the village they gave his hand burial in the churchyard where it is said to appear periodically, seeking reunion with the body of its owner. The second tale puts the trumpet-major into the Battle of

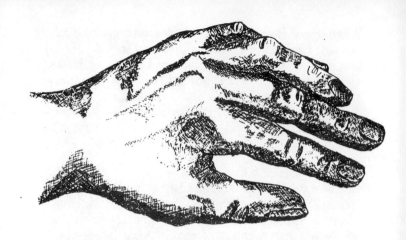

Chettle Common which took place well over a hundred years later on December 16th, 1780. This was an affray between poachers, of whom the trumpet-major was said to be one, and gamekeepers of the area. In it, the soldier lost his hand, although he did survive and go to London. The hand is said to appear in several places, the churchyard at Pimperne, Tarrant Hinton and Tarrant Gunville.

The Giant of Cerne Abbas

Nobody knows for certain how old the Cerne Giant is, nor indeed just who he is meant to represent, but like the White Horse of the poem, he is thought to be of great antiquity. He is first mentioned in books of the eighteenth century, but it is most likely that his virile masculinity dominated Trendle Hill, renamed Giant Hill, many years prior to that. From his appearance it is probable that he was connected with some sort of fertility rite. He strides the hill like a colossus, 180 feet high with shoulders 44 feet across. His 30 foot phallus does lend credence to the fertility theory but it has also been suggested that he could represent Hercules, or perhaps a little-known British prince Cernic. Another idea is that he might be

Ysbadadden, a mythical giant of Arthurian legend.

Stories abound as to his origins. One notion has it that he was carved by local either to embarrass the Abbot and monks of Cerne, or to draw attention to improper goings-on at the Abbey. At the time of the Reformation there were many such stories about religious houses. Another tale attributes the death of a real giant to the local farmers. Tired of losing sheep to the voracious appetite of the giant, they found him asleep one day after a particularly good feed of Cerne mutton and tied him down with stakes and ropes to the hillside where he lay. Then they killed him, and to comemmorate their deed, cut his outline into the grass. At certain times, it is thought, the figure assumes some kind of life and actually rises from the ground and marches down to the valley in search of water.

It is however, generally accepted that the figure is extremely ancient, probably dating from the Bronze age, and his particularly aggressive masculinity, taken together with the Maypole fertility rites that took place in the nearby Frying Pan, does appear to link him with some as yet unknown fertility cult.

The Mermaid of Church Ope Cove, Portland

From historical fact to a romantic tale from Hardy's Ilse of Slingers, Portland. A mermaid was supposed to have come ashore in Church Ope on the island one Sunday morning as the worthies of the place were going to worship. It is thought that she was taken into the church, but she died. The building now is a ruin and the churchyard is overgrown, but the story is still talked about ....

The Prophetess ,of Devon.

Joanna Southcott was a mysterious figure born in 1750 in the small Devon village of Gittisham near Ottery St. Mary. While young she worked as a domestic servant but was soon influenced by the touring evangelical methodist ministers, and soon set herself up as a preacher and forteller of the fortune, and started selling passports to heaven, for earthly money. Her personality soon attracted a considerable cult following. Some of her prophecies had been handed to a methodist minister, in a sealed envelope. The Reverend Pomeroy, no longer wishing to be associated with Joanna, burnt the envelopes. With the resulting fracas the sect labelled the Minister as the second Lucifer, and a representative of the Devil on Earth. Joanna issued a number of edicts to her followers, who numbered over 100,000. The men were forbidden to shave. The prophetess had also moved onto the greener pastures of Bristol and London, and ammassed a considerable fortune, from her own religion.

In her later years and shortly before her death she admitted her deception, though many still chose to believe in her.

The Dorset Ooser

There was a time, years ago, when no Dorset festival would have been complete without its Ooser. This was a person who capered about wearing the fierce, traditional mask resembling a bull, with bulbous staring eyes, huge teeth and a large set of bull horns. The last known old mask was taken from Melbury Osmond at the beginning of this century, but modern copies have been made since. Particularly on May Day, Celtic Beltane, the Ooser was a familiar sight in the villages of West Dorset, prancing around, trying his utmost to frighten onlookers. He was always among the crowds present at the maypole dancing in the Frying Pan. He could well be a link with the old Celtic god Cernunnos, the Horned One, known to the Romans as Pan.

WEATHERWISE

Weather forecasting rhymes, often based on centuries of observation and practical experience, abound in Old Wessex, although the following is highly unjust to our admirable clergy!

For a warm wet May
The parsons do pray,
For then death-fees
Do come their way.

In Devon there are many rhymes about the rain that keeps the grass so moist and lush.

If the ash before the oak
We shall surely get a soak.
If the oak before the ash
We shall only get a splash.

When the rain comes is important too, as the following couplet shows.

If is rains on Good Friday and Easter Day,
There will be plenty of grass but little good hay.

A mild winter would seem to be highly unpopular for several reasons.

A light (mild) Christmas, light harvest,
A green Christmas makes a fat churchyard.

Whilst —

A fog on the hill
Brings water to the mill.

And

If there is ice that will bear a duck before Martlemas,
There will be none that will bear a goose all winter.

(St. Martin's Day is on November 11th)

Cider is an important part of the life of the folk of Wessex, and the cider apple crop has always been regarded as one of the most important. In West Somerset and East Devon, May 21st was always viewed with some concern, the day of Culmstock Fair.

Till Culmstock Fair be come and gone
There may be apples or mid be none.

31

Are you superstitious? Do you touch wood to appease the spirits of the trees or refuse to walk under a ladder? Or do you perhaps regard our old legends and tales as nothing more than idle foolishness, stories to frighten children?

Whatever your opinion, surely nobody can deny that our heritage and our lives would be very much the poorer without our rich tapestry of 'old wives' tales'.

FISHERMENS' TALES

Witches were always reckoned a danger, on sea just as much as on land, and fishermen had their own ways of protecting themselves from the hazards of harmful spells.

Hagstones, that is ordinary stones with naturally formed holes through the middle, have long been regarded as protection against witches by fishermen in Dorset and Devon. These stones, hung beneath the gunwales of a boat, would give protection as no witch would attempt to interfere with a boat carrying one. In other lands, notably China, boats are decorated with painted eyes, 'oculi', in order to help them find their way in bad weather and sea danger ahead. There could well be a link between this idea and the protective hagstone of the West Country. Another defence that Dorset fishermen carry against witches is a mackerel pierced with a pin. This mackerel is kept in the locker whilst the boat is at sea.

Apart from its value as nourishment, fish also has a reputation for improving the virility of the eater. In Poole the Annual Sprat Supper was always a popular event, and one regular attender claimed that the fish did her husband good as each of their children was born exactly nine months after the supper! Unfortunately the birthrate in Poole seems to be declining now that Russian trawlers are causing a drastic reduction in the local catch!

There has always been a belief amongst seafaring men that a caul offers protection from drowning. Ideally, a babe should be born with it, but failing this, a bought one carried to sea would offer the same guarantee. As late as 1948 it was possible to purchase a caul in Poole for about £5.

ECHOES FROM THE PAST

Legends and ghost stories with links from the past abound in Wessex. Events like the escape of the Stuart King Charles II, the attempt of his natural son James Duke of Monmouth to seize the throne more than thirty years later, and Judge Jeffries and his notorious Bloody Assize, have become part of Wessex folk memory, lingering ghosts from years long gone. Yet occasionally a tale is told that brings back the old events, and reminds us once more of

'. . . . old unhappy far-off things,
and battles long ago.'

The Legend of the Screaming Skull

Bettiscombe Manor lies in the Vale of Marshwood in the western part of Dorset. It is here in the Manor that peace is kept by the presence of an ancient skull. Whilst it remains in the house there is quiet, but if it should be removed the building is shaken by screams and shudderings and the fate of all the inmates is in jeopardy until it is replaced. There have been a number of suggestions as to the origins of the skull, one actually linking it with the seventeenth century owner of Bettiscombe. In 1685 Azariah, the eldest son of the owner John Pinney, was condemned by Judge Jeffries for his part in the Monmouth Rebellion. He was sent to the West Indies as a slave but succeeded in making a fortune. One explanation of the presence of the skull is that it belonged to a negro slave owned by Azariah, and that the old man had declared that he would never rest until his body was returned to his native island for burial. Another suggests that it is the skull of a young woman murdered at Bettiscombe. However in 1963 the skull was examined by a professor from the Royal College of Surgeons who said it was probably the head of a young woman aged between twenty-five and thirty, of European rather than negro origin, and modern thought is inclined now to associate it with a nearby prehistoric site on Sliding Hill. There is a story that an early tenant of the farm threw the skull into the pond, but the disturbances in the house were so great that he went to great trouble to rake out the pond and return the skull to its proper place.

The Ghost of the Hanging Judge

The Great House in Broad Street, Lyme Regis lays claim to the ghost of the notorious Judge Jeffries. He is supposed to walk whenever the house is empty.

Jones' Chair

Throughout the Civil War in England, Lyme was staunchly Parliamentarian and Protestant when most of the West Country was for the King. Although beseiged by royalist forces, Lyme held on gallantly and the seige was eventually lifted. After the victory of Cromwell and his army, the town was congratulated for its bravery by the Parliamentary leaders. However, at the Restoration of King Charles II, persecution of Dissenters was restored and the installation of a particularly zealous Mayor of Lyme aroused a deal of local hatred.

Mayor Jones made it his business to discover any Dissenters in the area, and in order to carry out their worship in peace they had to go right outside Lyme. Services were held at White Chapel Rocks, Pinhay

Cliffs, and Jones found on the path through Ware Cliffs a kind of natural recess near to Chimney Rock where he could sit and observe the miscreants going to their forbidden prayers, and note their names for future prosecution. He was so hated that on his death the legend arose that the Devil took his body on board a ship leaving for the Mediterranean. When accosted, a spokesman shouted that the ship's captain was Satan, their destination was Mount Etna and the cargo was 'Old Jones'. At that point, the entire ship was said to have exploded into flames and disappeared, leaving behind the lingering smell of sulphur! Mayor Jones has earned for himself a lasting memorial in the folklore books!

Lawrence of Arabia

Clouds Hill, once the home of T. E. Lawrence, author of The Seven Pillars of Wisdom and famous as 'Lawrence of Arabia', is now in the care of the National Trust. On the roads outside the little house, local people have heard the sound of a ghostly motor cycle being driven at speed. It was while driving his Brough Superior motorcycle that Lawrence was killed in 1935.

The Horrors of Sandford Orcas

Sandford Orcas is a lovely Tudor manor house near Sherborne, and it has more than its fair share of ghosts. A monk who murdered his master in the main bedroom makes an annual appearance, and unidentified figures in the dress of long ago appear and disappear in the dining room and other parts of the building. There is thought to be the body of a young boy walled up behind the master bedroom by his mother, an early resident of the manor, and the smell of decaying flesh fills the area at odd times. On other occasions the smock-clad figure of a farmer appears. he hanged himself from a trap door in the house. The seven foot high ghost of a Georgian rapist who only appears to young women under twenty and a spectral

Red Lady are among the other supernatural visitors to Sandford Orcas. In all, it is thought that there are more than a dozen ghosts, and in 1966 a team from the BBC was sent to investigate what is called the most haunted house in England. One of the camera crew claimed that he had glimpsed the figure of the farmer, and in 1967 a team from the Paraphysical Laboratory at Downton made some investigations and reported that 'a reasonable prima facie case had been made out for the hauntings'.

The ghostly bells of Milton Abbas

When Joseph Damer, who later became Earl of Dorchester, came into the Milton estates in the eighteenth century, he did not like the view of the old village that he would see from his fine new mansion. So he ordered it to be flooded and a new village built out of sight of his splendid new home. But every year, on New Year's Eve, the anniversary of the flooding of the old village, the sound of bells echoes from beneath the waters of the lake.

WEST COUNTRY FESTIVALS Devon

May	Kingsteignton Ram Fair ... Whit Monday
June	ideford; Beating The Clock Race First week in June
July	Honiton; Hot Penny Ceremony & Fair ... Tuesday & Wednesday after July 19th
July	Exeter; Lammas Fair Tuesday before 3rd Wednesday in July
September	Barnstaple; St. Giles Fair ... Wednesday before September 20th
October	Tavistock; The Goose Fair ...... Second Wednesday in October
November	Shebbear, 'Turning The Devil's Boulder .. November 5th
November	Ottery St. Mary; The Running of The Barrels Halloween Night
November	Ashburton; Ale Tasting Festival November 26th

The Ram Fair Kingsteignton, Devon _ Whit Monday

A strange event that still uses an animal sacrifice to appease the Gods, though the ritual has been christianized. The carcass of a young ram is decorated with flowers and ribbons and paraded round the town, before it is eventually roasted and the pieces of meat sold to the waiting crowds. The ceremony would seem to predate the christian period a mixture of Spring fertility rites and animal sacrifice. A later story states that the town was suffering from a severe drought, the local priest and townsfolk prayed for relief, and a spring appeared near the church. The ram was roasted as an offering. A convenient story to explain an even older ceremony.

Beating The Clock Race, Bideford, Devon.

1st week in June

The Beating the Clock Race at Bideford is a modern event that occurs around the bridge that crosses the River Torridge. The bridge has twenty-four arches and the race across is started by the chimes of the parish clock that takes 21.8 seconds to strike eight. The object of the race is to cross the bridge before the final bell is struck.

Bideford also has an interesting witch story. In 1682 a woman called Termperence Lloyd was convicted of witchcraft along with two local accomplacies. Temperence was convicted of murdering by sorcery several local people in the area. She was eventually hung for her evil deeds.

Widecombe Fair, Devon. ___ Tuesday in September
The fair at Widecombe is not very old, although the song does mention a Tom Cobley, who was a local man who died in 1794. The first fair is recorded as occurring in 1850, to dispose of summer fat animals from the moor, especially ponies. Today it is much more of a public occasion, with fun fair and attractions and an established date in the West Country year.

Turning The Devil's Boulder, Shebbear (N.Devon)
November 5th
Shebbear is a small village in north Devon and has a curious custom that takes place each November. In the village square is a large red stone, on the evening of November the 5th, the near-by church rings the bells to warn away the spirits and Devil from the stone. The vicar then leads a group of men with ropes and crowbars who go down to the square and turn the stone, for if the stone is not turned each year then a catastrophe will strike the village.

In common with many of these stones the Devil is said to have dropped it on the village square, though how and why the custom to turn such a large stone started is a mystery and probably goes back to pre-christian times.

Ale Tasting at Ashburton in Devon.
26th November
Each winter the newly elected Portreeve or Mayor as he is now called is appointed. Under his patronage several other positions are also appointed, which are now more honorary than working. They include pig drivers, bread weighers, scavangers and official Ale Tasters. The Ale Taster has to go round all the inns in the town trying the beer. This he does with the other dignitaries. If the beer is found in good order he presents the Landlord with a sprig of evergreen, which is hung on the front door. I would presume after the tenth pub the chief Ale Taster is hung on the door.

Dorset

Easter	Corfe Castle; Shrove Tuesday Football.
Shrove Tuesday
May	Abbotsbury; Garland Day ..... May 13th
October	Pack Monday Fair Monday after Oct. 10th

Pack Monday Fair of Sherborne, Dorset.
October 10th each year

The Pack Monday Fair is held every year on October 10th. The fair would start with a march through the town, on the night before. An archaic group of musicians would gather blowing and banging a collection of makeshift instruments. In recent years the proceedings at night have got out of hand and have been curtailed by the police. The group of spontaneous musicians was known as 'Teddy Roe's Band'. The custom of the band and fair go back to 1490 when the Abbey at Sherborne was rebuilt after a fire. The maisons celebrated the completion of work by parading round the town and singing. The event became an annual celebration with a fair.

Somerset

January	Carhampton; Wassailing The Apple Trees
January 17th
May	Hobby Horse Fair .... May 1st
September	Frome; Cheese Fair .... Spetember
September	Bridgewater; St. Matthew's Fair ....
Wednesday before September 21st	
	Wednesday before September 21st
October	Hinton St. George; Punkie Night .... Last
Thursday in October
November	Bridgewater Carnival .... November 15th

The Hobby Horse Festival, Minehead, Somerset.
April 30th

On the evening of the 30th of April a ten foot long wooden framed hobby horse is paraded through the streets of Minehead. The hobby-horse is decorated with ribbons and a tail on the back, the effigy is carried by a single man, who dances and collects money. At one time the hobby-horse had two jesters who entered people's houses to collect their fee. There are a number of conflicting explanations for the custom and perhaps all have an element of truth. The oldest is that the event is part of a spring rite, the story is that during the dark ages Minehead was often sacked by Viking raiders. One day two local fisherman seeing a Viking fleet decided to make their boat look like a dragon. Their careful disguise scared off the raiders, and the resulting victory has been celebrated ever since.

Books on folklore are legion and it would be impossible to list them all. The following are among those to which I am particularly indebted.

Christmas Customs & Folklore	
Folklore of the Sea	Margaret Baker
Folklore of Plants	
Folklore of Devon	Ralph Whitlock
Somerset Folklore	R. L. Tongue
British Folklore, Myths & Legends	Marc Alexander
Exploring Ancient Dorset	George Osborn
Highways and Byways in Dorset	Sir F. Treves
Folklore Calendar	George Long
Dorset Folklore	Maureen Hymas
Customs & Traditions of England	Garry Hogg
Oral Folk Tales of Wessex	Kingsley Palmer
The Dorset Coastline	L. Pridham
Dorsetshire Folklore	Udal
Notes on Charmouth	R. W. J. Pavey